Reading Informational Texts:

Nonfiction Passages and Exercises
Based on the Common Core
State Standards

I

PRESTWICK HOUSE, INC.

"Proud to Be on the Teacher's Side"

Senior Editor:
Paul Moliken

Writers:
Magedah Shabo
Elizabeth Osborne

Cover and Text Design:
Maria J. Mendoza

Layout and Production:
Jeremy Clark

PRESTWICK HOUSE, INC.
"Everything for the English Classroom!"

Reading Informational Texts:
Nonfiction Passages and Exercises
Based on the Common Core
State Standards

I

TABLE OF CONTENTS

READING
SELECTIONS

Ernie Pyle:

The Death of Captain Waskow

INTRODUCTION

"The Death of Captain Waskow"

Henry T. Waskow was an American army captain during World War II. Waskow was born in 1918, and enlisted in the Texas Army National Guard with his two older brothers. By the time the US became involved in World War II, he had received training as a lieutenant and proved to be an officer who put his soldiers' welfare above all else. In 1943, while stationed in Italy, Waskow witnessed combat for the first time. On December 12th, as his unit was launching an attack, Waskow was hit with shrapnel, which lodged in his chest, killing him almost instantly.

When the captain's body was brought to a safe area, war correspondent Ernie Pyle witnessed Waskow's soldiers' emotional response, and he wrote the column, "The Death of Captain Waskow." The piece was not published until January 10, 1944, and has become one of Pyle's most famous works.

Ernie Pyle

Ernie Pyle was born on August 3, 1900, on a farm in rural Indiana. At the age of 18 he joined the Naval Reserve, but after World War I was over, he returned to his home state to study at Indiana University. Pyle spent three years at the university, but with only one semester left, he took a job at a small Indiana paper, where he worked for three months before moving to Washington, D.C., to work for *The Washington Daily News* as a reporter.

By 1935, Pyle had begun writing a national travel column for the Scripps-Howard Alliance group. Although Pyle enjoyed doing his own writing, he often suffered from depression and rarely seemed satisfied in his work.

In 1942, with America fighting in World War II, Pyle became a war columnist who focused on the life of the common combat soldier, a perspective that won him great fame and for which he was awarded the Pulitzer Prize. Pyle was killed in the Pacific on April 18, 1945, just a few months before the Japanese surrender. His most famous column is "The Death of Captain Waskow," and his works have been collected into four books.

The Death of Captain Waskow

AT THE FRONT LINES IN ITALY, January 10, 1944
In this war I have known a lot of officers who were loved and respected by the soldiers under them. But never have I crossed the trail of any man as beloved as Capt. Henry T. Waskow of Belton, Texas.

Capt. Waskow was a **company** commander in the 36th Division. He had led his company since long before it left the States. He was very young, only in his middle twenties, but he carried in him a sincerity and gentleness that made people want to be guided by him.

"After my own father, he came next," a sergeant told me.

"He always looked after us," a soldier said. "He'd go to bat for us every time."

"I've never knowed him to do anything unfair," another one said.

I was at the foot of the mule trail the night they brought Capt. Waskow's body down. The moon was nearly full at the time, and you could see far up the trail, and even part way across the valley below. Soldiers made shadows in the moonlight as they walked.

Dead men had been coming down the mountain all evening, lashed onto the backs of mules. They came lying belly-down across the wooden pack-saddles, their heads hanging down on the left side of the mule, their stiffened legs sticking out awkwardly from the other side, bobbing up and down as the mule walked.

The Italian **mule-skinners** were afraid to walk beside dead men, so Americans had to lead the mules down that night. Even the Americans were reluctant to unlash and lift off the bodies at the bottom, so an officer had to do it himself, and ask others to help.

The first one came early in the morning. They slid him down from the mule and stood him on his feet for a moment, while they got a new grip. In the half light he might have been merely a sick man standing there, leaning on the others. Then they laid him on the ground in the shadow of the low stone wall alongside the road.

I don't know who that first one was. You feel small in the presence of dead men, and ashamed at being alive, and you don't ask silly questions.

Pay attention to the way Pyle unfolds his description of Captain Waskow in the beginning of the article. Where does the narrative begin?

Why do you think Pyle describes the soldiers' bodies in such detail?

Why might the Italians have been "afraid to walk beside dead men"?

Why might Pyle have felt "ashamed at being alive"?

5

The scene is described with terms like "moonlight," "half light," and "shadow." Why might Pyle have chosen these descriptive terms?

We left him there beside the road, that first one, and we all went back into the cowshed and sat on water cans or lay on the straw, waiting for the next batch of mules.

Somebody said the dead soldier had been dead for four days, and then nobody said anything more about it. We talked soldier talk for an hour or more. The dead man lay all alone outside in the shadow of the low stone wall.

Then a soldier came into the cowshed and said there were some more bodies outside. We went out into the road. Four mules stood there, in the moonlight, in the road where the trail came down off the mountain. The soldiers who led them stood there waiting. "This one is Captain Waskow," one of them said quietly.

Pyle reinforces the somber and lonely tone of the scene through this description of bodies that "lie there in the shadows until somebody else comes after them."

Two men unlashed his body from the mule and lifted it off and laid it in the shadow beside the low stone wall. Other men took the other bodies off. Finally there were five lying end to end in a long row, alongside the road. You don't cover up dead men in the combat zone. They just lie there in the shadows until somebody else comes after them.

The unburdened mules moved off to their olive orchard. The men in the road seemed reluctant to leave. They stood around, and gradually one by one I could sense them moving close to Capt. Waskow's body. Not so much to look, I think, as to say something in finality to him, and to themselves. I stood close by and I could hear.

One soldier came and looked down, and he said out loud, "God damn it." That's all he said, and then he walked away. Another one came. He said, "God damn it to hell anyway." He looked down for a few last moments, and then he turned and left.

The officer calls Captain Waskow "old man" as a term of affection. This expression reminds the reader, however, that Waskow was merely in his mid-twenties when he died.

Another man came; I think he was an officer. It was hard to tell officers from men in the half light, for all were bearded and grimy dirty. The man looked down into the dead captain's face, and then he spoke directly to him, as though he were alive. He said: "I'm sorry, old man."

Then a soldier came and stood beside the officer, and bent over, and he too spoke to his dead captain, not in a whisper but awfully tenderly, and he said: "I sure am sorry, sir."

Then the first man squatted down, and he reached down and took the dead hand, and he sat there for a full five minutes, holding the dead hand in his own and looking intently into the dead face, and he never uttered a sound all the time he sat there.

And finally he put the hand down, and then reached up and gently straightened the points of the captain's shirt collar, and then he sort of rearranged the tattered edges of his uniform around the wound. And then he got up and walked away down the road in the moonlight, all alone.

After that the rest of us went back into the cowshed, leaving the five dead men lying in a line, end to end, in the shadow of the low stone wall. We lay down on the straw in the cowshed, and pretty soon we were all asleep.

Note the repetition of "and he" and "and then he" in these two paragraphs; this is an example of a rhetorical device called anaphora. What effect does the use of anaphora create in this passage?

Anaphora: the repetition of a word or group of words within a short section of writing.

Some reprints of this column left out the final paragraph. What impression does this paragraph leave with the reader? How would the tone of the article's ending have been different if this paragraph had been left out?

VOCABULARY

Note: All definitions are based on the context in which the term is used in this reading selection.

company: a unit of soldiers, usually commanded by a captain or major
mule-skinner: a person who drives mules, also known as a muleteer

EXERCISES

◎ Short-Answer Questions

Answer each of the following questions in a few sentences, based on the text you have just read. Briefly explain each of your answers.

1. Summarize the text in one paragraph. Be sure to include all of the author's main points.

2. Analyze how the author orders his ideas. How does he transition from one point to the next? How does this affect his argument?

3. Analyze the overall tone of this passage.

4. The author talks about the way the Italian and American mule-skinners unlashed the dead bodies from the mules. Explain how this paragraph develops the idea of status in this passage.

◎ Essay Question

Carefully read Ernie Pyle's "The Death of Captain Waskow" and write a well-organized essay analyzing Pyle's main purpose and his rhetorical strategies for reaching that purpose. What does Pyle desire for the reader to understand? Be sure to cite textual evidence to support your answer.

Harriet Jacobs:

Incidents in the Life of a Slave Girl
Chapters I-II ("Childhood" and "The New Master
and Mistress")

INTRODUCTION

Incidents in the Life of a Slave Girl

Incidents in the Life of a Slave Girl is one of several slave narratives published around the time of the Civil War to inform Northerners of slavery's evils. Escaped slave Harriet Jacobs wrote the memoir under the pseudonym Linda Brent and had it published in 1861, when she was 48 years old. At that time, the American Civil War was just beginning. The book was praised by members of the abolitionist movement, who were eager to end slavery. Among those less sympathetic to the abolitionist movement, however, *Incidents* was highly controversial for its openness about the sexual abuse of slaves. Many critics of the time also questioned the narrative's authorship, having a low opinion of the intellect and abilities of slaves, and doubting whether a female former slave could write so well.

Harriet Jacobs

Harriet Jacobs was born a slave in North Carolina in 1813. Despite being property in legal terms, Jacobs had a relatively easy and happy early life, living independently with her parents, who owned their own house. At the age of twelve, however, she became the property of a local doctor. Jacobs's memoir recounts the cruelty and sexual harassment she suffered at this master's hands—not least of which was his interference in her intended marriage with a local freedman. Her relationship with her first love severed, Jacobs eventually became involved with a white lawyer and bore him two children, whom he raised apart from her. Jacobs spent several years in hiding in the tight confines of her grandmother's attic before escaping to the North, where she lived out the rest of her life. Jacobs died in 1897 and is buried in Massachusetts.

Incidents in the Life of a Slave Girl
Chapter I: Childhood

I was born a slave; but I never knew it till six years of happy childhood had passed away. My father was a carpenter, and considered so intelligent and skillful in his trade, that, when buildings out of the common line were to be erected, he was sent for from long distances, to be head workman. On condition of paying his mistress two hundred dollars a year, and supporting himself, he was allowed to work at his trade, and manage his own affairs. His strongest wish was to purchase his children; but, though he several times offered his hard earnings for that purpose, he never succeeded. In complexion my parents were a light shade of brownish yellow, and were termed **mulattoes**. They lived together in a comfortable home; and, though we were all slaves, I was so fondly shielded that I never dreamed I was a piece of merchandise, trusted to them for safe keeping, and **liable** to be demanded of them at any moment. I had one brother, William, who was two years younger than myself—a bright, affectionate child. I had also a great treasure in my maternal grandmother, who was a remarkable woman in many respects. She was the daughter of a planter in South Carolina, who, at his death, left her mother and his three children free, with money to go to St. Augustine, where they had relatives. It was during the Revolutionary War; and they were captured on their passage, carried back, and sold to different purchasers. Such was the story my grandmother used to tell me; but I do not remember all the particulars. She was a little girl when she was captured and sold to the keeper of a large hotel. I have often heard her tell how hard she fared during childhood. But as she grew older she **evinced** so much intelligence, and was so faithful, that her master and mistress could not help seeing it was for their interest to take care of such a valuable piece of property. She became an indispensable personage in the household, officiating in all capacities, from cook and wet nurse to seamstress. She was much praised for her cooking; and her rice crackers became so famous in the neighborhood that many people were **desirous** of obtaining them. In consequence of

Describe the tone of the first paragraph. After you've read the rest of the narrative, discuss how the tone changes over the course of the text, and how this change contributes to Jacobs's overall purpose.

How does Jacobs' description of her family members defy misperceptions about slaves that were common in her time?

Here, Jacobs introduces the idea that masters often had sexual relations with female slaves and then enslaved the children born from these unions.

Describe Jacobs's language in this sentence. How does the tone of this sentence contribute to her purpose in writing the narrative?

Jacobs describes Benjamin's appearance as "nearly white." What effect would this description have likely had on Northern readers?

$720 in Jacobs's time would equate to approximately $18,000 in today's dollars. This detail helps illustrate the incredible financial incentive Southerners had for perpetuating slavery.

What does this exclamation imply about slaveholders?

How does Jacobs further develop her characterization of her grandmother in this passage?

numerous requests of this kind, she asked permission of her mistress to bake crackers at night, after all the household work was done; and she obtained leave to do it, provided she would clothe herself and her children from the profits. Upon these terms, after working hard all day for her mistress, she began her midnight bakings, assisted by her two oldest children. The business proved profitable; and each year she laid by a little, which was saved for a fund to purchase her children. Her master died, and the property was divided among his heirs. The widow had her dower in the hotel which she continued to keep open. My grandmother remained in her service as a slave; but her children were divided among her master's children. As she had five, Benjamin, the youngest one, was sold, in order that each heir might have an equal portion of dollars and cents. There was so little difference in our ages that he seemed more like my brother than my uncle. He was a bright, handsome lad, nearly white; for he inherited the complexion my grandmother had derived from Anglo-Saxon ancestors.

Though only ten years old, seven hundred and twenty dollars were paid for him. His sale was a terrible blow to my grandmother, but she was naturally hopeful, and she went to work with renewed energy, trusting in time to be able to purchase some of her children. She had laid up three hundred dollars, which her mistress one day begged as a loan, promising to pay her soon. The reader probably knows that no promise or writing given to a slave is legally binding; for, according to Southern laws, a slave, *being* property, can *hold* no property. When my grandmother lent her hard earnings to her mistress, she trusted solely to her honor. The honor of a slaveholder to a slave!

To this good grandmother I was indebted for many comforts. My brother Willie and I often received portions of the crackers, cakes, and preserves, she made to sell; and after we ceased to be children we were indebted to her for many more important services.

Such were the unusually fortunate circumstances of my early childhood. When I was six years old, my mother died; and then, for the first time, I learned, by the talk around me, that I was a slave. My mother's mistress was the daughter of my grandmother's mistress. She was the foster sister of my mother; they were both nourished at my grandmother's breast. In fact, my mother had been weaned at three months old, that the babe of the mistress might obtain sufficient food. They played together as children; and, when they became women, my mother was a most faithful servant to her whiter foster sister. On her death-bed her mistress promised that her children should never suffer for anything; and during her lifetime she kept her word. They all spoke kindly of my dead mother, who had been a slave merely in name, but in nature was noble and womanly. I grieved for her, and my young mind was troubled with the thought who would now take care of me and my little brother. I was told that my home was now to be with her mistress; and I found it a happy one. No **toilsome** or disagreeable duties were imposed on me. My mistress was so kind to me that I was always glad to do her bidding, and proud to labor for her as much as my young years would permit. I would sit by her side for hours, sewing diligently, with a heart as free from care as that of any free-born white child. When she thought I was tired, she would send me out to run and jump; and away I bounded, to gather berries or flowers to decorate her room. Those were happy days—too happy to last. The slave child had no thought for the morrow; but there came that blight, which too surely waits on every human being born to be a **chattel**.

When I was nearly twelve years old, my kind mistress sickened and died. As I saw the cheek grow paler, and the eye more glassy, how earnestly I prayed in my heart that she might live! I loved her; for she had been almost like a mother to me. My prayers were not answered. She died, and they buried her in the little churchyard, where, day after day, my tears fell upon her grave.

I was sent to spend a week with my grandmother. I was now old enough to begin to think of the future; and again and again I asked myself what they would do with me. I felt sure I should never find another mistress so kind as the one who was gone. She had promised my dying mother that her children should never suffer for anything; and when I remembered that, and recalled

Why might Jacobs have included this detail?

Which of the work's themes is conveyed in this sentence?

her many proofs of attachment to me, I could not help having some hopes that she had left me free. My friends were almost certain it would be so. They thought she would be sure to do it, on account of my mother's love and faithful service. But, alas! we all know that the memory of a faithful slave does not **avail** much to save her children from the auction block.

> *What surprising fact is revealed in this sentence, and what effect would it likely have had on Northern readers?*

After a brief period of suspense, the will of my mistress was read, and we learned that she had **bequeathed** me to her sister's daughter, a child of five years old. So vanished our hopes. My mistress had taught me the **precepts** of God's Word: "Thou shalt love thy neighbor as thyself." "Whatsoever ye would that men should do unto you, do ye even so unto them." But I was her slave,

> *What rhetorical purpose do these Bible verses (the first of which originates in Leviticus 19:18 and the second of which is from Matthew 7:12) serve?*

and I suppose she did not recognize me as her neighbor. I would give much to blot out from my memory that one great wrong. As a child, I loved my mistress; and, looking back on the happy days I spent with her, I try to think with less bitterness of this act of injustice. While I was with her, she taught me to read and spell; and for this privilege, which so rarely falls to the lot of a slave, I bless her memory.

She possessed but few slaves; and at her death those were all distributed among her relatives. Five of them were my grandmother's children, and had shared the same milk that nourished her mother's children. Notwithstanding my grandmother's long and faithful service to her owners, not one of her children escaped the auction block. These God-breathing machines are no more, in the sight of their masters, than the cotton they plant, or the horses they tend.

Chapter II: The New Master and Mistress

Dr. Flint, a physician in the neighborhood, had married the sister of my mistress, and I was now the property of their little daughter. It was not without murmuring that I prepared for my new home; and what added to my unhappiness, was the fact that my brother William was purchased by the same family. My father, by his nature, as well as by the habit of transacting business as a skillful mechanic, had more of the feelings of a freeman than is common among slaves. My brother was a spirited boy;

> *The phrase "It was not without murmuring that I prepared for my new home" is an example of litotes.*
>
> ***Litotes**: a deliberate understatement in which an idea is expressed through the negation of its opposite*
>
> *This comment suggests that Jacobs did, in fact, complain quite a bit about her circumstances.*

and being brought up under such influences, he daily detested the name of master and mistress. One day, when his father and his mistress both happened to call him at the same time, he hesitated between the two; being perplexed to know which had the strongest claim upon his obedience. He finally concluded to go to his mistress. When my father **reproved** him for it, he said, "You both called me, and I didn't know which I ought to go to first."

"You are *my* child," replied our father, "and when I call you, you should come immediately, if you have to pass through fire and water."

Poor Willie! He was now to learn his first lesson of obedience to a master. Grandmother tried to cheer us with hopeful words, and they found an echo in the **credulous** hearts of youth.

When we entered our new home we encountered cold looks, cold words, and cold treatment. We were glad when the night came. On my narrow bed I moaned and wept, I felt so desolate and alone.

I had been there nearly a year, when a dear little friend of mine was buried. I heard her mother sob, as the clods fell on the coffin of her only child, and I turned away from the grave, feeling thankful that I still had something left to love. I met my grandmother, who said, "Come with me, Linda"; and from her tone I knew that something sad had happened. She led me apart from the people, and then said, "My child, your father is dead." Dead! How could I believe it? He had died so suddenly I had not even heard that he was sick. I went home with my grandmother. My heart rebelled against God, who had taken from me mother, father, mistress, and friend. The good grandmother tried to comfort me. "Who knows the ways of God?" said she. "Perhaps they have been kindly taken from the evil days to come." Years afterwards I often thought of this. She promised to be a mother to her grandchildren, so far as she might be permitted to do so; and strengthened by her love, I returned to my master's. I thought I should be allowed to go to my father's house the next morning; but I was ordered to go for flowers, that my mistress's house might be decorated for an evening party. I spent

Throughout her story, Jacobs demonstrates some of the ways in which slaveholders would weaken and override healthy familial bonds among slaves.

What purpose does the anaphora serve in this sentence?

Anaphora: repetition of a word or group of words within a short section of writing.

How do these interjections convey Jacobs's state of mind?

the day gathering flowers and weaving them into **festoons**, while the dead body of my father was lying within a mile of me. What cared my owners for that? he was merely a piece of property. Moreover, they thought he had spoiled his children, by teaching them to feel that they were human beings. This was **blasphemous** doctrine for a slave to teach; **presumptuous** in him, and dangerous to the masters.

The next day I followed his remains to a humble grave beside that of my dear mother. There were those who knew my father's worth, and respected his memory.

My home now seemed more dreary than ever. The laugh of the little slave-children sounded harsh and cruel. It was selfish to feel so about the joy of others. My brother moved about with a very grave face. I tried to comfort him, by saying, "Take courage, Willie; brighter days will come by and by."

"You don't know anything about it, Linda," he replied. "We shall have to stay here all our days; we shall never be free."

I argued that we were growing older and stronger, and that perhaps we might, before long, be allowed to hire our own time, and then we could earn money to buy our freedom. William declared this was much easier to say than to do; moreover, he did not intend to *buy* his freedom. We held daily controversies upon this subject.

Little attention was paid to the slaves' meals in Dr. Flint's house. If they could catch a bit of food while it was going, well and good. I gave myself no trouble on that score, for on my various errands I passed my grandmother's house, where there was always something to spare for me. I was frequently threatened with punishment if I stopped there; and my grandmother, to avoid detaining me, often stood at the gate with something for my breakfast or dinner. I was indebted to *her* for all my comforts, spiritual or **temporal**. It was *her* labor that supplied my scanty wardrobe. I have a vivid recollection of the linsey-woolsey dress given me every winter by Mrs. Flint. How I hated it! It was one of the badges of slavery.

While my grandmother was thus helping to support me from her hard earnings, the three hundred dollars

What does Jacobs imply by saying that William "did not intend to *buy* his freedom"?

What does Jacobs mean by the word "controversies" here? Does this word have the same meaning in modern speech?

she had lent her mistress were never repaid. When her mistress died, her son-in-law, Dr. Flint, was appointed executor. When grandmother applied to him for payment, he said the estate was **insolvent**, and the law prohibited payment. It did not, however, prohibit him from retaining the silver candelabra, which had been purchased with that money. I presume they will be handed down in the family, from generation to generation.

My grandmother's mistress had always promised her that, at her death, she should be free; and it was said that in her will she made good the promise. But when the estate was settled, Dr. Flint told the faithful old servant that, under existing circumstances, it was necessary she should be sold.

On the appointed day, the customary advertisement was posted up, proclaiming that there would be a "public sale of negroes, horses, &c." Dr. Flint called to tell my grandmother that he was unwilling to wound her feelings by putting her up at auction, and that he would prefer to dispose of her at private sale. My grandmother saw through his hypocrisy; she understood very well that he was ashamed of the job. She was a very spirited woman, and if he was **base** enough to sell her, when her mistress intended she should be free, she was determined the public should know it. She had for a long time supplied many families with crackers and preserves; consequently, "Aunt Marthy," as she was called, was generally known, and every body who knew her respected her intelligence and good character. Her long and faithful service in the family was also well known, and the intention of her mistress to leave her free. When the day of sale came, she took her place among the chattels, and at the first call she sprang upon the auction block. Many voices called out, "Shame! Shame! Who is going to sell *you*, Aunt Marthy? Don't stand there! That is no place for *you*." Without saying a word, she quietly awaited her fate. No one bid for her. At last, a feeble voice said, "Fifty dollars." It came from a maiden lady, seventy years old, the sister of my grandmother's deceased mistress. She had lived forty years under the same roof with my grandmother; she

Why might Jacobs have included these exclamations from the crowd in her description of the sale of Aunt Marthy?

knew how faithfully she had served her owners, and how cruelly she had been defrauded of her rights; and she resolved to protect her. The auctioneer waited for a higher bid; but her wishes were respected; no one bid above her. She could neither read nor write; and when the bill of sale was made out, she signed it with a cross. But what consequence was that, when she had a big heart overflowing with human kindness? She gave the old servant her freedom.

At that time, my grandmother was just fifty years old. Laborious years had passed since then; and now my brother and I were slaves to the man who had **defrauded** her of her money, and tried to defraud her of her freedom. One of my mother's sisters, called Aunt Nancy, was also a slave in his family. She was a kind, good aunt to me; and supplied the place of both housekeeper and waiting maid to her mistress. She was, in fact, at the beginning and end of everything.

Mrs. Flint, like many southern women, was totally deficient in energy. She had not strength to **superintend** her household affairs; but her nerves were so strong, that she could sit in her easy chair and see a woman whipped, till the blood trickled from every stroke of the lash. She was a member of the church; but partaking of the Lord's supper did not seem to put her in a Christian frame of mind. If dinner was not served at the exact time on that particular Sunday, she would station herself in the kitchen, and wait till it was dished, and then spit in all the kettles and pans that had been used for cooking. She did this to prevent the cook and her children from eking out their meagre fare with the remains of the gravy and other scrapings. The slaves could get nothing to eat except what she chose to give them. Provisions were weighed out by the pound and ounce, three times a day. I can assure you she gave them no chance to eat wheat bread from her flour barrel. She knew how many biscuits a quart of flour would make, and exactly what size they ought to be.

Dr. Flint was an **epicure**. The cook never sent a dinner to his table without fear and trembling; for if there happened to be a dish not to his liking, he would either order her to be whipped, or compel her to eat

Jacobs again points out the hypocrisy endemic in slaveholders who identified with Christianity, yet were cruel to their slaves.

every mouthful of it in his presence. The poor, hungry creature might not have objected to eating it; but she did object to having her master cram it down her throat till she choked.

They had a pet dog that was a nuisance in the house. The cook was ordered to make some Indian mush for him. He refused to eat, and when his head was held over it, the froth flowed from his mouth into the basin. He died a few minutes after. When Dr. Flint came in, he said the mush had not been well cooked, and that was the reason the animal would not eat it. He sent for the cook, and compelled her to eat it. He thought that the woman's stomach was stronger than the dog's; but her sufferings afterwards proved that he was mistaken. This poor woman endured many cruelties from her master and mistress; sometimes she was locked up, away from her nursing baby, for a whole day and night.

When I had been in the family a few weeks, one of the plantation slaves was brought to town, by order of his master. It was near night when he arrived, and Dr. Flint ordered him to be taken to the work house, and tied up to the joist, so that his feet would just escape the ground. In that situation he was to wait till the doctor had taken his tea. I shall never forget that night. Never before, in my life, had I heard hundreds of blows fall, in succession, on a human being. His piteous groans, and his "O, pray don't, massa," rang in my ear for months afterwards. There were many **conjectures** as to the cause of this terrible punishment. Some said master accused him of stealing corn; others said the slave had quarreled with his wife, in presence of the overseer, and had accused his master of being the father of her child. They were both black, and the child was very fair.

I went into the work house next morning, and saw the cowhide still wet with blood, and the boards all covered with gore. The poor man lived, and continued to quarrel with his wife. A few months afterwards Dr. Flint handed them both over to a slave-trader. The guilty man put their value into his pocket, and had the satisfaction of knowing that they were out of sight and hearing. When the mother was delivered into the trader's hands, she said. "You *promised* to treat me well."

Why might it have been a crime for female slaves to identify the fathers of their children?

To which he replied, "You have let your tongue run too far; damn you!" She had forgotten that it was a crime for a slave to tell who was the father of her child.

From others than the master persecution also comes in such cases. I once saw a young slave girl dying soon after the birth of a child nearly white. In her agony she cried out, "O Lord, come and take me!" Her mistress stood by, and mocked at her like an **incarnate** fiend. "You suffer, do you?" she exclaimed. "I am glad of it. You deserve it all, and more too."

The girl's mother said, "The baby is dead, thank God; and I hope my poor child will soon be in heaven, too."

"Heaven!" retorted the mistress. "There is no such place for the like of her and her bastard."

The poor mother turned away, sobbing. Her dying daughter called her, feebly, and as she bent over her, I heard her say, "Don't grieve so, mother; God knows all about it; and HE will have mercy upon me."

Her sufferings, afterwards, became so intense, that her mistress felt unable to stay; but when she left the room, the scornful smile was still on her lips. Seven children called her mother. The poor black woman had but the one child, whose eyes she saw closing in death, while she thanked God for taking her away from the greater bitterness of life.

VOCABULARY

Note: All definitions are based on the context in which the term is used in this reading selection.

avail: to help; to benefit
base: without honor or morality
bequeathed: to have left something to someone else, usually in a will
blasphemous: sacrilegious against God or religion; profane, disrespectful
chattel: an item of personal property
conjectures: opinions or judgments of something based on too little information
credulous: willing to believe or trust too easily
defrauded: deceived; illegally obtained by means of deception
desirous: having a desire or want for something
epicure: a person who takes pleasure in food and drink
evinced: to have shown or demonstrated; revealed
festoons: chains or garlands of flowers
incarnate: embodied or present in human form
insolvent: unable to pay debts
liable: likely
mulattoes: people of mixed white and black ancestry
precepts: rules or principles of action
presumptuous: overstepping normal boundaries or taking liberties with established practices
reproved: to have voiced disapproval of something or someone
superintend: to be responsible for the management of something; to oversee
temporal: worldly or material, as opposed to spiritual
toilsome: involving tedious or hard work

EXERCISES

Short-Answer Questions

Answer each of the following questions in a few sentences, based on the text you have just read. Briefly explain each of your answers.

1. What is Jacobs's purpose in writing this memoir? Use evidence from the text to support your answer.

2. Based on the reading selections from *Incidents in the Life of a Slave Girl*, what do you think Jacobs would say is the primary evil of slavery?

3. How does Jacobs use rhetorical devices in the first two chapters of *Incidents*? Support your answer with specific examples from the text.

4. How does Jacobs develop the character of her grandmother? Use details from the text to support your answer.

Essay Question

How does Jacobs detail her developing consciousness of her own condition as a slave? Use evidence from the text to support your answer.

Patrick Henry:

Speech to the Second Virginia Convention

INTRODUCTION

Speech to the Second Virginia Convention

Patrick Henry delivered this address in Richmond in the spring of 1775, at the second of five special conventions that served as an interim government for Virginia during the revolutionary period. Attendees of the convention included George Washington, who would become the nation's first president, and Thomas Jefferson, the primary author of the Declaration of Independence and future third president of the United States.

Through this speech, Henry is credited with having convinced the Virginia House of Burgesses to arm Virginia's troops in preparation for the American Revolutionary War.

The exact text of the speech Henry delivered to the convention has not been preserved. What remains of the speech today is a re-creation based on the accounts of witnesses who attended the convention. In 1816, seventeen years after Henry's death, biographer William Wirt published this version of the speech in his book *Sketches of the Life and Character of Patrick Henry*.

Patrick Henry's speech to the Second Virginia Convention is best known for its famous concluding line: "Give me liberty or give me death!"

Patrick Henry

Patrick Henry was a major figure in the American Revolutionary War and is considered one of the nation's founding fathers. Known as a great orator, Henry is most famous for his speech to the Second Virginia Convention, which appears in the following pages. Henry played a vital role in promoting the Revolutionary War and the republican model of government. He was a member of the First Continental Congress, held in 1774, and also served two nonconsecutive terms as Governor of Virginia.

After the Revolutionary War, Henry led the Anti-Federalist movement, which opposed the replacement of the Articles of Confederation with the US Constitution. The Articles of Confederation, which governed the states from 1777 through 1788, placed greater limits on the federal government than did the Constitution. Afraid that the adoption of the Constitution would jeopardize states' rights and individual liberties, Henry voted against ratification in 1788. The passion for freedom and independence that drove this and many of Henry's other political decisions can be seen vividly in his famous 1775 speech.

Speech to the Second Virginia Convention

No man thinks more highly than I do of the patriotism, as well as abilities, of the very worthy gentlemen who have just addressed the House. But different men often see the same subject in different lights; and, therefore, I hope it will not be thought disrespectful to those gentlemen, if, entertaining as I do opinions of a character very opposite to theirs, I shall speak forth my sentiments freely and without reserve. This is no time for **ceremony**.

The question before the House is one of awful moment to this country. For my own part, I consider it as nothing less than a question of freedom or slavery; and in proportion to the magnitude of the subject ought to be the freedom of the debate. It is only in this way that we can hope to arrive at truth, and fulfill the great responsibility which we hold to God and our country. Should I keep back my opinions at such a time, through fear of giving offense, I should consider myself as guilty of treason toward my country, and of an act of disloyalty toward the Majesty of Heaven, which I **revere** above all earthly kings.

Mr. President, it is natural to man to indulge in the illusions of hope. We are apt to shut our eyes against a painful truth, and listen to the song of that **siren**, till she transforms us into beasts. Is this the part of wise men, engaged in a great and **arduous** struggle for liberty? Are we disposed to be of the number of those, who, having eyes, see not, and having ears, hear not, the things which so nearly concern their **temporal** salvation? For my part, whatever anguish of spirit it may cost, I am willing to know the whole truth; to know the worst, and to provide for it.

I have but one lamp by which my feet are guided, and that is the lamp of experience. I know of no way of judging of the future but by the past. And judging by the past, I wish to know what there has been in the conduct of the British ministry for the last ten years to justify those hopes with which gentlemen have been pleased to **solace** themselves and the House. Is it that **insidious** smile with which our petition has been lately received? Trust it not, sir; it will prove a snare to your feet. Suffer not yourselves

What does the expression "awful moment" mean in this context?

This is one of several examples of *allusion* in the speech.

Henry alludes to the sirens of Greek mythology, who were powerful creatures, often depicted as women with bird-like wings; their songs entranced sailors and led them into danger.

Allusion: a reference to a person, place, poem, book, event, etc., that the author expects the reader will recognize

This particular passage alludes to Mark 8:18, which says, "**Having eyes do you not see, and having ears do you not hear?** And do you not remember?"

As you read, consider the effect Henry's biblical and classical allusions would have had on his audience.

In this passage, Henry borrows the imagery of Job 18:8, which reads, "For he is cast into a net by his own feet, and he **walketh upon a snare**."

The expression "betrayed with a kiss" alludes to the betrayal of Jesus by Judas. In the biblical account, after betraying Jesus to those who would kill him, Judas greeted him with a kiss as the way of identifying to the Romans exactly who he was.

This passage contains an example of procatalepsis.

Procatalepsis: a rhetorical device in which the speaker anticipates and responds to possible objections to his or her argument

As you read Henry's argument, consider the effect this technique creates.

Henry uses forms of the words "supplication" and "remonstrance" multiple times. What do these words mean? How do these two approaches differ? How do they compare with the alternate approach Henry urges his audience to take at the end of the following paragraph?

The phrases "prostrated ourselves before the throne" and "from the foot of the throne" describe the position Henry believes the American Colonists currently hold in relation to the British monarchy. What does it mean to "prostrate" oneself? What image does Henry create in this passage, and what effect was it intended to have on his audience?

to be betrayed with a kiss. Ask yourselves how this gracious reception of our petition comports with those warlike preparations which cover our waters and darken our land. Are fleets and armies necessary to a work of love and **reconciliation**? Have we shown ourselves so unwilling to be reconciled that force must be called in to win back our love? Let us not deceive ourselves, sir. These are the implements of war and **subjugation**; the last arguments to which kings resort.

I ask gentlemen, sir, what means this martial array, if its purpose be not to force us to submission? Can gentlemen assign any other possible motive for it? Has Great Britain any enemy in this quarter of the world to call for all this accumulation of navies and armies? No, sir, she has none. They are meant for us: they can be meant for no other. They are sent over to bind and **rivet** upon us those chains which the British ministry have been so long forging. And what have we to oppose to them? Shall we try argument? Sir, we have been trying that for the last ten years. Have we anything new to offer upon the subject? Nothing. We have held the subject up in every light of which it is capable; but it has been all in vain.

Shall we resort to entreaty and humble **supplication**? What terms shall we find which have not been already exhausted? Let us not, I **beseech** you, sir, deceive ourselves longer. Sir, we have done everything that could be done, to avert the storm which is now coming on. We have petitioned; we have **remonstrated**; we have supplicated; we have **prostrated** ourselves before the throne, and have **implored** its **interposition** to arrest the tyrannical hands of the ministry and Parliament. Our petitions have been slighted; our remonstrances have produced additional violence and insult; our supplications have been disregarded, and we have been spurned, with contempt, from the foot of the throne!

In vain, after these things, may we indulge the fond hope of peace and reconciliation. There is no longer any room for hope. If we wish to be free—if we mean to preserve **inviolate** those inestimable privileges for which we have been so long contending—if we mean not **basely** to abandon the noble struggle in which we have been so long engaged, and which we have pledged ourselves never to abandon, until the glorious object of our contest shall be obtained—we must fight! I repeat it, sir, we must fight! An appeal to arms and to the God of Hosts is all that is left us!

They tell us, sir, that we are weak—unable to cope with so **formidable** an **adversary**. But when shall we be stronger? Will it be the next week, or the next year? Will it be when we are totally disarmed, and when a British guard shall be stationed in every house? Shall we gather strength by **irresolution** and inaction? Shall we acquire the means of effectual resistance by lying **supinely** on our backs and hugging the **delusive** phantom of hope, until our enemies shall have bound us hand and foot?

Sir, we are not weak if we make a proper use of those means which the God of nature has placed in our power. Three millions of people armed in the holy cause of liberty, and in such a country as that which we possess, are invincible by any force which our enemy can send against us. Besides, sir, we shall not fight our battles alone. There is a just God who **presides** over the destinies of nations, and who will raise up friends to fight our battles for us. The battle, sir, is not to the strong alone; it is to the **vigilant**, the active, the brave. Besides, sir, we have no election. If we were base enough to desire it, it is now too late to retire from the contest. There is no retreat but in submission and slavery! Our chains are forged! Their clanking may be heard on the plains of Boston! The war is inevitable—and let it come! I repeat it, sir, let it come!

It is in vain, sir, to **extenuate** the matter. Gentlemen may cry, "Peace, peace!"—but there is no peace. The war is actually begun! The next gale that sweeps from the north will bring to our ears the clash of resounding arms! Our **brethren** are already in the field! Why stand we here idle? What is it that gentlemen wish? What would they have? Is life so dear, or peace so sweet, as to be purchased at the price of chains and slavery? Forbid it, Almighty God! I know not what course others may take; but as for me, give me liberty or give me death!

Henry uses a series of rhetorical questions in this paragraph. What is their intended effect on the audience?

Rhetorical Question: a figure of speech used for its persuasive effect; a question to which the speaker does not expect a reply

The word "election," as used here, simply means "choice."

This is another biblical allusion. (Jeremiah 6:14 reads, "They have healed also the hurt of the daughter of my people slightly, **saying, 'Peace, peace,' when there is no peace**.")

Henry uses more rhetorical questions in this passage. Describe their probable effect on the audience.

What is the overall mood of this speech?

VOCABULARY

Note: All definitions are based on the context in which the term is used in this reading selection.

adversary: an opponent or competitor
arduous: difficult or tiring
basely: in an immoral or dishonorable manner
beseech: to ask someone urgently to do something, to plead
brethren: people who belong to a particular group, usually a profession, society, or religion
ceremony: a formality; a social gesture or act having little significance
delusive: deceptive, misleading
extenuate: to lessen the magnitude of something, usually by giving excuses
formidable: impressive; commanding respect, fear, or awe
implored: asked urgently; pleaded
insidious: harmfully enticing; treacherous
interposition: the act of placing oneself between two things
inviolate: free from injury or violation
irresolution: the state of being unsure how to proceed or continue; indecision
presides: holds a position of authority
prostrated: laid flat on the ground, face down, as in submission
reconciliation: the act of reestablishing a cordial relationship
remonstrated: protested; objected; argued against
revere: to feel great respect or admiration for something
rivet: to fasten or hold securely
siren: a female creature in Greek mythology whose singing lured sailors to crash their ships on the rocks
solace: to comfort or console
subjugation: forced submission or control
supinely: with the face upward
supplication: a prayer for assistance or a bid for help
temporal: worldly or material, as opposed to spiritual
vigilant: watchful; wary; alert

EXERCISES

Short-Answer Questions

Answer each of the following questions in a few sentences, based on the text you have just read. Briefly explain each of your answers.

1. What is Henry's primary purpose in delivering this speech? Quote specific passages in which Henry makes his intentions clear.

2. What are the main points of Henry's argument? Cite specific passages to support your answer.

3. In the beginning of the speech, Henry makes the following comment:

> "No man thinks more highly than I do of the patriotism, as well as abilities, of the very worthy gentlemen who have just addressed the House. But different men often see the same subject in different lights; and, therefore, I hope it will not be thought disrespectful to those gentlemen if, entertaining as I do, opinions of a character very opposite to theirs, I shall speak forth my sentiments freely and without reserve."

Drawing inferences from this passage and from the rest of the text, explain the position taken by the people who spoke before Patrick Henry at the convention. Provide examples from the text where necessary.

4. Describe Henry's use of rhetorical questions. What purpose do they seem to serve in the speech?

5. What effect does Henry achieve with his use of procatalepsis and allusion?

Essay Question

Write a response to Henry's speech from the perspective of a member of Virginia's House of Burgesses. In your response, argue against the position Henry has presented. Incorporate a summary of Henry's argument into your response, analyzing its strengths and weaknesses and pointing out any factual or logical errors it contains. Be sure to use direct quotes from the speech in your response.

John Fitzgerald Kennedy:

1961 Inaugural Address

INTRODUCTION

1961 Inaugural Address

In the Constitution, the only mention of an inauguration is that the winner of the election must make an oath or a declaration before actually *becoming* the president of the United States. The Twentieth Amendment, passed in 1933, made the date of inauguration January 20, but up to that point, inaugurations took place on March 4. The incoming president might have a crisis develop during those months, however, as Lincoln did with the secession of the South, and as Franklin Roosevelt did during the Great Depression.

It is customary for presidents not to actually write their own speeches, but to work on the final form after instructing others on the main points to be covered, and the 1961 inaugural speech is no different. Kennedy wanted a short speech, one that looked toward the future, but did not ignore the past.

Coming in the middle of the twentieth century, during which American dominance was unquestioned—the country had been instrumental in bringing World Wars I and II to successful conclusions—the popular national sentiment was that the United States was the envy of the world, and its influence should be spread. However, there were hints of social and international upheavals, and it was necessary for Kennedy to strike the right tone, one of confidence and assurance, but also one of reaching out to other countries. In addition, children born just before and during WWII were coming of age in huge numbers, and he had to appeal to them.

Many historians, as well as people who study rhetoric, consider Kennedy's one of the best inauguration speeches ever written.

John Fitzgerald Kennedy

John Fitzgerald Kennedy, the thirty-fifth president of the United States, was born May 29, 1917, in Brookline, Massachusetts. His father, Joseph P. Kennedy, Sr., had served as Ambassador to Britain and was a multimillionaire. Kennedy's mother, Rose, was the daughter of a prominent Boston politician. They encouraged their children to enter public service, and John, or Jack as he was called, after a distinguished term in the Navy in WWII, was elected to the US House of Representatives in 1946 and to the US Senate in 1952.

In 1960, Kennedy ran for the presidency and defeated Richard Nixon, his Republican opponent,. However, prior to the victory, Kennedy had to overcome several obstacles, one of which was his religion, Roman Catholicism. A Catholic had never been elected to the presidency, and his religion caused concern among many citizens; in a speech while campaigning, Kennedy faced this challenge directly and defused it.

After a highly energized campaign and following the first televised presidential debates, Kennedy won the election; he became, at 43, the youngest person elected to the office and began his term of office when he delivered this speech on January 20, 1961.

Significantly, Kennedy took office from Dwight Eisenhower, the oldest president up to that point, and the contrasts between age and youth are alluded to at various times in the speech.

Kennedy's presidency began in a time of heightened rhetoric and deep philosophical and governmental differences between the world's two superpowers, the US and the Soviet Union, both of which possessed enough nuclear weapons to destroy the world. In addition, mounting racial tensions in the United States would dominate much of his domestic policy.

In April of 1961, a US-sponsored invasion to oust Fidel Castro, the Russian-backed Cuban president, failed. Then, in August 1961, the Soviets began to build the Berlin Wall, further increasing tensions between East and West. The next year, spy planes from the United States took photographs of Soviet missile installations being built in Cuba. Kennedy declared that he would blockade the island and board any ship headed toward it. The Russian premier, Nikita Khrushchev, finally ordered the sites dismantled, probably preventing a nuclear confrontation. Because of his determination, Kennedy's approval soared, both in the US and abroad. Additionally, perceptions of Kennedy were changed because he seemed to be the equal of more experienced world leaders, and in 1963, a test ban treaty was signed, greatly limiting the testing of nuclear weapons.

In addition to foreign issues, much of Kennedy's time in office centered on domestic policy. Soon after he established the Peace Corps, which sends American citizens to underdeveloped countries, and he championed the Apollo moon program. Racial discrimination in the United States, however, would force Kennedy to deal with important crises in civil rights. Politically, civil rights was a difficult topic, but circumstances, including the murder of civil rights protestors, gave Kennedy the impetus to push for legislation that would grant equal access to public schools, restaurants, housing, and voting rights for all citizens, regardless of race.

On November 22, 1963, on a political trip to Dallas, Texas, Kennedy was assassinated. He had been president 1,036 days.

1961 Inaugural Address

Vice President Johnson, Mr. Speaker, Mr. Chief Justice, President Eisenhower, Vice President Nixon, President Truman, reverend clergy, fellow citizens:

We observe today not a victory of party, but a celebration of freedom—symbolizing an end, as well as a beginning—**signifying** renewal, as well as change. For I have sworn before you and Almighty God the same **solemn** oath our forebears prescribed nearly a century and three-quarters ago.

The world is very different now. For man holds in his mortal hands the power to **abolish** all forms of human poverty and all forms of human life. And yet the same revolutionary beliefs for which our **forebears** fought are still at issue around the globe—the belief that the rights of man come not from the generosity of the state, but from the hand of God.

We dare not forget today that we are the heirs of that first revolution. Let the word go forth from this time and place, to friend and foe alike, that the torch has been passed to a new generation of Americans—born in this century, **tempered** by war, disciplined by a hard and bitter peace, proud of our ancient heritage, and unwilling to witness or permit the slow undoing of those human rights to which this nation has always been committed, and to which we are committed today, at home and around the world.

Let every nation know, whether it wishes us well or ill, that we shall pay any price, bear any burden, meet any hardship, support any friend, oppose any foe, to assure the survival and the success of liberty.

This much we pledge—and more.

To those old allies whose cultural and spiritual origins we share, we pledge the loyalty of faithful friends. United there is little we cannot do in a **host** of cooperative ventures. Divided there is little we can do—for we dare not meet a powerful challenge at odds and split **asunder**.

To those new states whom we welcome to the ranks of the free, we pledge our word that one form of colonial control shall not have passed away merely to be replaced by a far more iron tyranny. We shall not always expect to find them supporting our view. But we shall

Kennedy pairs words that have opposite meanings—for example, "end" and "beginning." Locate other examples of this technique in the speech.

To what is Kennedy alluding when he says that man has the power to "abolish…all forms of human life"?

How does this first short sentence prepare the audience for the forceful lengthy one that follows?

Kennedy has set out his first main point.

In 1946, Winston Churchill referred to the Soviet Union as "The Iron Curtain."

always hope to find them strongly supporting their own freedom—and to remember that, in the past, those who foolishly sought power by riding the back of the tiger ended up inside.

To those people in the huts and villages of half the globe struggling to break the bonds of mass misery, we pledge our best efforts to help them help themselves, for whatever period is required—not because the Communists may be doing it, not because we seek their votes, but because it is right. If a free society cannot help the many who are poor, it cannot save the few who are rich.

To our sister republics south of our border, we offer a special pledge: to convert our good words into good deeds, in a new alliance for progress, to assist free men and free governments in casting off the chains of poverty. But this peaceful revolution of hope cannot become the prey of hostile powers. Let all our neighbors know that we shall join with them to oppose aggression or **subversion** anywhere in the Americas. And let every other power know that this hemisphere intends to remain the master of its own house.

To that world assembly of **sovereign** states, the United Nations, our last best hope in an age where the instruments of war have far outpaced the instruments of peace, we renew our pledge of support—to prevent it from becoming merely a forum for **invective**, to strengthen its shield of the new and the weak, and to enlarge the area in which its **writ** may run.

Finally, to those nations who would make themselves our adversary, we offer not a pledge but a request: that both sides begin anew the quest for peace, before the dark powers of destruction unleashed by science **engulf** all humanity in planned or accidental self-destruction.

We dare not tempt them with weakness. For only when our arms are sufficient beyond doubt can we be certain beyond doubt that they will never be employed.

But neither can two great and powerful groups of nations take comfort from our present course—both sides overburdened by the cost of modern weapons, both rightly alarmed by the steady spread of the deadly atom, yet both racing to alter that uncertain balance of terror that **stays** the hand of mankind's final war.

This humorous imagery is borrowed from a Chinese proverb, which translates, "He who rides a tiger is afraid to dismount." What do the tiger and its rider represent in Kennedy's speech, and what message is he trying to send to other nations through this metaphor?

Metaphor: an implicit comparison between two unlike things

In a perfect construction that uses the technique of antithesis, Kennedy juxtaposes *many* with *few*, and *rich* with *poor*.

Antithesis: a rhetorical device that emphasizes opposites.

This statement alludes to the Monroe Doctrine, the policy that the United States should essentially be "master" of affairs within the Western Hemisphere, without interference from Europe or other Old World powers.

Kennedy refers to advances in nuclear weapons technology, which were developing more rapidly than were scientific advances in other fields during this era.

What is the meaning of this paragraph? Summarize Kennedy's point in your own words.

The word "us" is used only once before this paragraph, but it is used eleven times between now and the end of the speech. What might Kennedy have intended to emphasize with his repeated use of the word "us"?

What have been the main points of Kennedy's argument up to this point?

This biblical allusion is taken from Isaiah 58:6. By invoking this particular comment, Kennedy is asking other countries, especially the Soviet Union, to allow the people they control to have more freedom. He continues this theme in the next two paragraphs.

Kennedy alludes to events of World War II in this description. The US army attacked the Nazis from the *beachheads* of Normandy and pushed the Japanese from *jungles* on islands in the Pacific.

Kennedy uses polysyndeton to link phrases in paragraphs 20 and 21. What is the effect of using polysyndeton in this sentence?

Polysyndeton: the repetition of conjunctions in a series for stylistic effect

Kennedy now begins the third main thrust of the speech.

This biblical allusion is from Romans 12:12

Kennedy uses two rhetorical questions to more intimately involve his listening audience. These are the only two questions in the speech.

Rhetorical Question: a question used for its persuasive effect; a question to which the speaker does not expect a reply

So let us begin anew—remembering on both sides that **civility** is not a sign of weakness, and sincerity is always subject to proof. Let us never negotiate out of fear, but let us never fear to negotiate.

Let both sides explore what problems unite us instead of **belaboring** those problems which divide us.

Let both sides, for the first time, formulate serious and precise proposals for the inspection and control of arms, and bring the absolute power to destroy other nations under the absolute control of all nations.

Let both sides seek to invoke the wonders of science instead of its terrors. Together let us explore the stars, conquer the deserts, **eradicate** disease, tap the ocean depths, and encourage the arts and commerce.

Let both sides unite to heed, in all corners of the earth, the command of Isaiah—to "undo the heavy burdens, and [to] let the oppressed go free."

And, if a beachhead of cooperation may push back the jungle of suspicion, let both sides join in creating a new endeavor—not a new balance of power, but a new world of law—where the strong are just, and the weak secure, and the peace preserved.

All this will not be finished in the first one hundred days. Nor will it be finished in the first one thousand days; nor in the life of this Administration; nor even perhaps in our lifetime on this planet. But let us begin.

In your hands, my fellow citizens, more than mine, will rest the final success or failure of our course. Since this country was founded, each generation of Americans has been summoned to give testimony to its national loyalty. The graves of young Americans who answered the call to service surround the globe.

Now the trumpet summons us again—not as a call to bear arms, though arms we need—not as a call to battle, though embattled we are—but a call to bear the burden of a long twilight struggle, year in and year out, "rejoicing in hope; patient in **tribulation**," a struggle against the common enemies of man: tyranny, poverty, disease, and war itself.

Can we forge against these enemies a grand and global alliance, North and South, East and West, that can assure a more fruitful life for all mankind? Will you join in that historic effort?

In the long history of the world, only a few generations have been granted the role of defending freedom in its hour of maximum danger. I do not shrink from this responsibility—I welcome it. I do not believe that any of us would exchange places with any other people or any other generation. The energy, the faith, the devotion which we bring to this endeavor will light our country and all who serve it. And the glow from that fire can truly light the world.

And so, my fellow Americans, ask not what your country can do for you; ask what you can do for your country.

My fellow citizens of the world, ask not what America will do for you, but what together we can do for the freedom of man.

Finally, whether you are citizens of America or citizens of the world, ask of us here the same high standards of strength and sacrifice which we ask of you. With a good conscience our only sure reward, with history the final judge of our deeds, let us go forth to lead the land we love, asking His blessing and His help, but knowing that here on earth God's work must truly be our own.

In the most famous line of the speech, Kennedy makes the citizens of the United States responsible for the future of the country and of the world. He exhorts people not to be passive recipients of the largesse of government, but to become involved in improving the state of the world.

VOCABULARY

Note: All definitions are based on the context in which the term is used in this reading selection.

abolish: to eliminate; to get rid of
asunder: apart; split into parts or pieces
belaboring: continuing to discuss or deal with an issue
civility: courtesy
engulf: to enclose, surround, or overwhelm
eradicate: to eliminate; to completely remove
forebears: ancestors; previous generations
host: a very large number; many
invective: abusive language; insults
signifying: indicating; meaning
solemn: important; having a tradition or ceremony
sovereign: independent
stays: inhibits; stops
subversion: efforts toward overthrowing a government
tempered: hardened; strengthened
tribulation: difficulty; distress
writ: a legal authority

EXERCISES

Short-Answer Questions

Answer each of the following questions in a few sentences, based on the text you have just read. Briefly explain each of your answers.

1. What do you think are Kennedy's main points? How does he develop them? Find specific sentences or passages that show what they are.

2. What is the explicit meaning of paragraph five? Based on what Kennedy says in that paragraph, how do you think he would have reacted to the terrorist attacks of Sept. 11, 2001?

3. Look at the entire speech and explain how Kennedy introduces the topic of the dangers of nuclear weapons, expands on their potential dangers, and offers solutions relating to them.

4. Throughout the speech, Kennedy uses opposites to make his points. Evaluate how successful this technique is. How might this rhetorical approach have affected his audience?

Essay Question

Throughout Kennedy's inaugural speech, he refers to Russia without mentioning the country by name. Reply to Kennedy in a letter from the perspective of Nikita Khrushchev, who was the premier of the Soviet Union during Kennedy's presidency. Respond to Kennedy's points, agreeing with some and providing arguments against others. You may need to do some research into the Cold War at the time Kennedy was inaugurated, as well as finding out information about Khrushchev himself.

Margaret Chase Smith:

*Remarks to the Senate in Support of a
Declaration of Conscience*

INTRODUCTION

Remarks to the Senate in Support of Declaration of Conscience

Margaret Chase Smith's "Declaration of Conscience" speech was delivered on the floor of the Senate on June 1, 1950. It is addressed to the official presiding over the Senate. The object of Senator Smith's criticism in the speech is Senator Joseph McCarthy of Wisconsin. McCarthy was responsible for a series of investigations of alleged Communists working for the State Department. He was later censured by the Senate for some of his actions during these investigations.

Margaret Chase Smith

Margaret Chase Smith was born in 1897 in Skowhegan, Maine. She married Clyde Smith, a Maine politician, in 1930. In 1937, Clyde Smith was elected to the House of Representatives, but within only a few years, he became ill from a serious heart condition. After his death in 1940, Margaret Chase Smith ran for his seat and won. In 1948, she was elected to the Senate.

Smith's famous "Declaration of Conscience" speech was given during the period after World War II, when the United States began to get involved in what would become known as the "Cold War" with the Soviet Union. The two countries were competing to gain a technological advantage, especially with regard to nuclear weapons. As such, there was widespread suspicion in the United States regarding Communist infiltration and spying. Senator McCarthy's "Wheeling Speech," given in early 1950, named individuals in the State Department who were allegedly members of the Communist Party. (The term "McCarthyism" was later coined to describe the practice of accusing individuals of disloyalty or crimes against the government without adequate evidence.) In the preceding years, the House Un-American Activities Committee, formed to investigate Communist infiltration, had accused a long list of civilians, including individuals in the movie industry, of being Communists. Senator Smith gave her "Declaration of Conscience" speech in 1950 to protest the actions of the Committee and McCarthy.

In the years following Smith's speech, McCarthy lost some of his power and popularity. Smith served as a senator until she was defeated in the 1972 Maine senatorial election by William Hathaway. Following her congressional tenure, she returned to Maine. The Margaret Chase Smith Library in Skowhegan, Maine, contains her political papers and other important documents. She remains one of the longest-serving female senators in the history of the United States.

Remarks to the Senate in Support of a Declaration of Conscience

Statement of Senator Margaret Chase Smith

Mr. President:

I would like to speak briefly and simply about a serious national condition. It is a national feeling of fear and frustration that could result in national suicide and the end of everything that we Americans hold dear. It is a condition that comes from the lack of effective leadership in either the legislative branch or the executive branch of our Government.

That leadership is so lacking that serious and responsible proposals are being made that national advisory commissions be appointed to provide such critically needed leadership.

I speak as briefly as possible because too much harm has already been done with irresponsible words of bitterness and selfish political **opportunism**. I speak as simply as possible because the issue is too great to be **obscured** by **eloquence**. I speak simply and briefly in the hope that my words will be taken to heart.

I speak as a Republican, I speak as a woman. I speak as a United States Senator. I speak as an American.

The United States Senate has long enjoyed worldwide respect as the greatest **deliberative** body in the world. But recently that deliberative character has too often been **debased** to the level of a forum of hate and character assassination sheltered by the shield of **congressional immunity**.

It is ironical that we Senators can in debate in the Senate directly or indirectly, by any form of words **impute** to any American, who is not a Senator, any conduct or motive unworthy or unbecoming an American—and without that non-Senator American having any legal **redress** against us—yet if we say the same thing in the Senate about our colleagues we can be stopped on the grounds of being out of order.

It is strange that we can verbally attack anyone else without restraint and with full protection and yet we hold ourselves above the same type of criticism here on

Smith is addressing her remarks to the president pro tempore of the Senate.

What does Smith mean by the expression "national suicide"?

How does Smith introduce the idea of speech as a potential force for harm, and how does this idea relate to the main topic of her speech?

Why might Smith have enumerated each of these categories to which she belongs?

What is the main idea of this section?

What is Smith's point in this paragraph?

the Senate Floor. Surely the United States Senate is big enough to take self-criticism and self-**appraisal**. Surely we should be able to take the same kind of character attacks that we dish out to outsiders.

> What central idea of the speech does Smith develop here?

I think that it is high time for the United States Senate and its members to do some soul searching—for us to weigh our consciences—on the manner in which we are performing our duty to the people of America—on the manner in which we are using or abusing our individual powers and privileges.

I think that it is high time that we remembered that we have sworn to uphold and defend the Constitution.

> How does Smith relate the concept of the constitutional right to a fair trial to the question of McCarthyism?

I think that it is high time that we remembered that the Constitution, as amended, speaks not only of the freedom of speech but also of trial by jury instead of trial by accusation.

Whether it be a criminal prosecution in court or a character prosecution in the Senate, there is little practical distinction when the life of a person has been ruined.

> This may be a reference to Senator Joseph McCarthy of Wisconsin, who, six months before this speech, had accused several members of the State Department, by name, of being Communists.

Those of us who shout the loudest about Americanism in making character assassinations are all too frequently those who, by our own words and acts, ignore some of the basic principles of Americanism—

The right to criticize;

The right to hold unpopular beliefs;

The right to protest;

The right of independent thought.

The exercise of these rights should not cost one single American citizen his reputation or his right to a livelihood nor should he be in danger of losing his reputation or livelihood merely because he happens to know someone who holds unpopular beliefs. Who of us doesn't? Otherwise none of us could call our souls our own. Otherwise thought control would have set in.

The American people are sick and tired of being afraid to speak their minds lest they be politically smeared as "Communists" or "Fascists" by their opponents. Freedom of speech is not what it used to be in America. It has been so abused by some that it is not exercised by others. The American people are sick and tired of seeing innocent people smeared and guilty people whitewashed. But there have been enough proved cases to cause nationwide distrust and strong suspicion that there may be something to the unproved, sensational accusations.

As a Republican, I say to my colleagues on this side of the aisle that the Republican Party faces a challenge today that is not unlike the challenge that it faced back in Lincoln's day. The Republican Party so successfully met that challenge that it emerged from the Civil War as the champion of a united nation—in addition to being a Party that **unrelentingly** fought loose spending and loose programs.

Today our country is being psychologically divided by the confusion and the suspicions that are bred in the United States Senate to spread like cancerous tentacles of "know nothing, suspect everything" attitudes. Today we have a Democratic Administration that has developed a **mania** for loose spending and loose programs. History is repeating itself—and the Republican Party again has the opportunity to emerge as the champion of unity and prudence.

The record of the present Democratic Administration has provided us with sufficient campaign issues without the necessity of resorting to political smears. America is rapidly losing its position as leader of the world simply because the Democratic Administration has pitifully failed to provide effective leadership.

The Democratic Administration has completely confused the American people by its daily contradictory grave warnings and optimistic assurances—that show the people that our Democratic Administration has no idea of where it is going.

The Democratic Administration has greatly lost the confidence of the American people by its complacency to the threat of communism here at home and the leak of vital secrets to Russia through key officials of the Democratic Administration. There are enough proved cases to make this point without diluting our criticism with unproved charges.

Surely these are sufficient reasons to make it clear to the American people that it is time for a change and that a Republican victory is necessary to the security of this

What earlier organizational structure is Smith developing here?

Why does Smith bring in this comparison?

What is Smith's sub-argument here, and how is it related to the main argument?

country. Surely it is clear that this nation will continue to suffer as long as it is governed by the present ineffective Democratic Administration.

Yet to displace it with a Republican regime embracing a philosophy that lacks political integrity or intellectual honesty would prove equally disastrous to this nation. The nation sorely needs a Republican victory. But I don't want to see the Republican Party ride to political victory on the Four Horsemen of **Calumny**—Fear, Ignorance, Bigotry and Smear.

I doubt if the Republican Party could—simply because I don't believe the American people will uphold any political party that puts political exploitation above national interest. Surely we Republicans aren't that desperate for victory.

I don't want to see the Republican Party win that way. While it might be a fleeting victory for the Republican Party, it would be a more lasting defeat for the American people. Surely it would ultimately be suicide for the Republican Party and the two-party system that has protected our American liberties from the dictatorship of a one party system.

As members of the Minority Party, we do not have the primary authority to formulate the policy of our Government. But we do have the responsibility of **rendering** constructive criticism, of clarifying issues, of **allaying** fears by acting as responsible citizens.

As a woman, I wonder how the mothers, wives, sisters and daughters feel about the way in which members of their families have been politically mangled in Senate debate—and I use the word 'debate' advisedly.

As a United States Senator, I am not proud of the way in which the Senate has been made a publicity platform for irresponsible **sensationalism**. I am not proud of the reckless abandon in which unproved charges have been hurled from this side of the aisle. I am not proud of the obviously staged, undignified countercharges that have been attempted in retaliation from the other side of the aisle.

I don't like the way the Senate has been made a **rendezvous** for **vilification**, for selfish political gain at the sacrifice of individual reputations and national

This is an allusion to the Four Horsemen of the Apocalypse mentioned in the Book of Revelation, often identified as Conquest, War, Famine, and Pestilence.

How does this further refine the idea of American values introduced earlier in the speech?

unity. I am not proud of the way we smear outsiders from the Floor of the Senate and hide behind the cloak of congressional immunity and still place ourselves beyond criticism on the Floor of the Senate.

As an American, I am shocked at the way Republicans and Democrats alike are playing directly into the Communist design of "confuse, divide and conquer." As an American, I don't want a Democratic Administration "white wash" or "cover up" any more than I want a Republican smear or witch hunt.

As an American, I condemn a Republican "Fascist" just as much as I condemn a Democrat "Communist." I condemn a Democrat "Fascist" just as much as I condemn a Republican "Communist." They are equally dangerous to you and me and to our country. As an American, I want to see our nation recapture the strength and unity it once had when we fought the enemy instead of ourselves.

It is with these thoughts I have drafted what I call a "Declaration of Conscience." I am gratified that Senator Tobey, Senator Aiken, Senator Morse, Senator Ives, Senator Thye and Senator Hendrickson, have **concurred** in that declaration and have authorized me to announce their concurrence.

VOCABULARY

Note: All definitions are based on the context in which the term is used in this reading selection.

allaying: putting to rest
appraisal: an evaluation
calumny: slander
concurred: agreed
congressional immunity: the exemption of Senators and Representatives from being arrested or prosecuted for any speech or debate that takes place in Congress
debased: brought down; ruined
deliberative: characterized by debate
eloquence: smooth and graceful language
impute: to attribute
mania: an obsession
obscured: made unclear
opportunism: the tendency or practice of prioritizing personal advantage
redress: way to obtain justice
rendering: producing
rendezvous: a meeting place
sensationalism: the practice of stirring up emotions through provocative language
unrelentingly: in a manner that does not give up
vilification: a verbal attack

EXERCISES

Short-Answer Questions

Answer each of the following questions in a few sentences, based on the text you have just read. Briefly explain each of your answers.

1. Smith does not explicitly mention the event or trend that has prompted her speech. Why might she have chosen not to identify those responsible for the events she criticizes?

2. How does Smith support her argument by appealing to the moral condition of the United States?

3. Explain how Smith ties the "lack of effective leadership" by the Democratic government to the "witch hunt" for Communists.

4. Explain the central idea of the speech. Use evidence from the text to support your explanation.

5. Explain how Smith structures the "Declaration of Conscience" speech.

◎ Essay Question

Analyze Smith's development of the idea that speech and language can be both positive and negative forces in her speech to the Senate.

NASA:

Light Emitting Diodes Bring Relief
to Young Cancer Patients

INTRODUCTION

NASA and "Light Emitting Diodes Bring Relief to Young Cancer Patients"

The National Aeronautics and Space Administration (NASA) was founded in 1958, during the time of the "Space Race," when the United States and the Soviet Union were competing against one another in developing technology to explore space. NASA would eventually be the agency responsible for both manned and unmanned space flights. Its major projects would include the Apollo program, which landed men on the Moon; the Mars Rover; the Space Shuttle program; the International Space Station; the Hubble Space Telescope; and interplanetary probes that have provided extensive information on conditions in the solar system. In addition, as the following article demonstrates, NASA supports research that leads to technological breakthroughs in science and medicine.

NASA publishes articles to inform the public of some of the many ways in which its research has proved useful for everyday life. In this article, readers learn how technology NASA developed for use in space is now being used to treat disease patients.

Light Emitting Diodes Bring Relief to Young Cancer Patients

NASA Technology used for Plant Growth Now in Clinical Trials

A device using specialized **light emitting diodes**, based on NASA technology for plant growth in space, is continuing to show promise as a treatment to aid healing of bone marrow transplant patients. Use of the LED apparatus has advanced to the second phase of clinical trials in US and foreign hospitals. Results from the first round of tests were highly encouraging, prompting researchers to expand the trials as they seek approval for the treatment as a standard of care for oral **mucositis**.

What is the main idea of the article, as introduced here?

A nurse holds a strange-looking device, moving it slowly toward a young patient's face. The note-card-sized device is covered with glowing red lights, but as it comes closer, the youngster shows no fear. He's hopeful this painless procedure using an array of lights will help ease or prevent some of the pain and discomfort associated with cancer treatment.

What is the purpose of this paragraph?

The youngster is participating in the second phase of human clinical trials for this light healing device. The first round of tests by Medical College of Wisconsin researchers at Children's Hospital of Wisconsin in Milwaukee was so encouraging that doctors have expanded the trials to several US and foreign hospitals.

"We've already seen how using LEDs can improve a bone marrow transplant patient's quality of life," said Dr. Harry Whelan, professor of **neurology**, **pediatrics** and **hyperbaric** medicine at the Medical College of Wisconsin in Milwaukee. "These trials will hopefully help us take the next steps to provide this as a standard of care for this ailment."

The light is produced by light emitting diodes, or LEDs. They are used in hundreds of applications, from electronic clock displays to jumbo TV screens.

How does the author expand upon the idea from paragraph one?

These LEDs provide light for plants grown on the Space Station as part of commercial experiments sponsored by industry under the Space Product Development Program at NASA's Marshall Space Flight Center in Huntsville, Ala. Researchers discovered that the diodes also had many promising medical applications, prompting this research to be funded by a NASA Small Business Innovation Research contract through the Technology Transfer Department at the Marshall Center.

Judging by paragraph seven, who is likely the intended audience for this article?

Biologists have found that cells exposed to near-**infrared** light—that is, energy just outside the visible range—from LEDs grow 150 to 200 percent faster than those cells not **stimulated** by such light. The light arrays increase energy inside cells that speeds up the healing process.

The article has explained the original use of the LEDs in plant growth, as well as their medical use. From this information, what inference can we make about the connection between plants and human cells?

In the first stage of the study, use of the LEDs resulted in significant relief to pediatric bone marrow transplant patients suffering the ravages of oral mucositis, a common side effect of **chemotherapy** and radiation treatments according to Dr. David Margolis, associate professor of pediatrics at the Medical College. He works with Dr. Whelan on the study at Children's Hospital of Wisconsin, a major teaching **affiliate** of the Medical College.

The article has explained that chemotherapy and radiation cause oral mucositis. We also know that infrared light is used to heal cells in patients suffering from oral mucositis. What can be inferred about the effects of chemotherapy and radiation on human cells?

Many times young bone marrow transplant recipients contract this condition that produces ulcerations in the mouth and throat, severe pain, and in some cases, inflammation of the entire gastro-intestinal tract. Swelling and bleeding occur, and chewing and swallowing become difficult, if not impossible—affecting a child's overall health because of reduced drinking and eating.

"Our first study was very encouraging, and using the LED device greatly reduced or prevented the mucositis problem, which is so painful and devastating to these children," said Whelan. "But we still need to learn more. We're conducting further clinical trials with larger groups and expanded control groups, as required by the US Food and Drug Administration, before the device can be approved and available for widespread use."

The clinical trials are expected to take approximately three years with a total of 80 patients. Participants currently include the Medical College of Wisconsin in Milwaukee; Roswell Park Cancer Institute in Buffalo, N.Y. and Instituto de Oncologia Pediatrica, in Sao Paulo, Brazil. Rush-Presbyterian-St. Luke's Medical Center in Chicago; University of Illinois Medical Center in

Chicago; Hospital Sirio Libanes in Sao Paulo Brazil; and Hadassah University Medical Center in Jerusalem, Israel have also asked to join the multi-center study.

In the first **clinical** study, the team examined each patient's mouth, tongue and throat. They asked the patient to rate the current level of pain before treatment. Each patient received one minute of LED therapy starting the day of the bone marrow transplant and a one-minute treatment each day thereafter for a two-week period.

The treatment device was a 3-by-5-inch portable, flat **array** of light emitting diodes. It was held on the outside of a patient's left cheek for just over a minute each day. The process was repeated over the patient's right cheek, but with foil placed between the LED array and the patient to provide a sham treatment for comparison. There wasn't any treatment of the throat area, which provided the **control** for the first study.

How does this paragraph refine the imagery introduced in paragraph two?

The researchers compared the percentage of patients with **ulcerative** oral mucositis to historical **epidemiological** controls. Just 53 percent of the treated patients in the bone marrow transplant group developed mucositis, considerably less than the usual rate of 70-90 percent. Patients also reported pain reduction in their mouths when compared to untreated pain seven days following bone marrow transplant.

What does the author mean by "historical epidemiological controls"? (Note: The words "epidemiological" and "control" are both defined in the vocabulary section at the end of the article.)

Quantum Devices of Barneveld, Wis., makes the wound-healing LED device. The company specializes in the manufacture of silicon **photodiodes—semiconductor** devices used for light detection—and light emitting diodes for commercial, industrial and medical applications.

VOCABULARY

Note: All definitions are based on the context in which the term is used in this reading selection.

affiliate: a member; an associate

array: an arrangement

chemotherapy: the use of chemicals as medicine to treat cancer

clinical: based on observation of a patient in a medical study

control: in a scientific experiment, an element or group that is used for comparison to other elements or groups

epidemiological: related to the branch of medicine that studies how diseases move within and across populations

hyperbaric: relating to how the human body processes oxygen at high atmospheric pressure

infrared: a spectrum of light invisible to the naked eye

light emitting diodes (LEDs): electronic devices that emit light when an electric current flows through them

mucositis: an inflammation of the mucous membranes

neurology: the branch of medicine dealing with the brain and nervous system

pediatrics: the branch of medicine concerned with children's health

photodiodes: devices that can convert light into voltage

semiconductor: a substance that allows electricity to travel through it; used in many modern electronic devices

stimulated: made active

ulcerative: causing sores

EXERCISES

◎ Short-Answer Questions

Answer each of the following questions in a few sentences, based on the text you have just read. Briefly explain each of your answers.

1. What kind of audience does the article appear to have been written for? Give evidence to support your answer.

2. How does the author of the article use quotations to develop the main idea?

3. How does the author introduce LEDs and explain what they are over the course of the article?

4. What is the tone of this article? Explain how the words the author uses contribute to this tone.

5. From the information in the passage, make an inference about why LEDs have the ability to speed up healing.

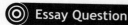

Essay Question

Explain how the words in this article contribute to the scientific purpose of the piece. Cite specific examples of how some of the terms used in the article have a different meaning in the context of science than they do in ordinary speech.

Justice Frank Murphy:

Dissenting Opinion in the Case of
Korematsu v. United States

INTRODUCTION

Justice Murphy's Dissenting Opinion in the Case of *Korematsu v. United States*

The United States entered World War II on December 7, 1941, following the attack on the naval base at Pearl Harbor, Hawaii, by Japanese forces. Fears of domestic spies and saboteurs working for the Japanese government against the United States became widespread, especially in California. In 1942, responding to these fears, President Franklin Roosevelt signed Executive Order 9066, which authorized military leaders to set up military zones from which they could choose to exclude people they considered security risks.

Exclusion Order No. 34, to which Judge Murphy refers in his argument, was one order that fell under Executive Order 9066. Military authorities issued an order excluding all persons of Japanese descent—whether American citizens or not—from areas along the Pacific coast. Citizens of Italian and German descent were also interned, since Germany and Italy were also enemies of the United States.

Fred Korematsu was an American citizen of Japanese descent who refused to report to a detention center in 1942 when General John L. DeWitt ordered all Japanese Americans to report to certain specified areas as a prelude to detention in camps.

In the case entitled *Korematsu v. United States*, the Supreme Court ruled 6-3 in favor of the government. This case was handed down in 1944.

Korematsu's conviction for not obeying the order was later overturned because of problems with the evidence submitted, but the Supreme Court has never reversed its decision in favor of the United States.

Frank Murphy

Associate Supreme Court Justice Frank Murphy was born in 1890 in Michigan. Following his graduation from the University of Michigan Law School, he held a variety of positions, including US District Attorney in Michigan and Mayor of Detroit. As Mayor, he was an ally of President Roosevelt and helped put some of Roosevelt's reforms into motion. In the 1930s, in recompense for Murphy's support, the president appointed him to several different positions in the Philippines. He was Governor of Michigan from 1937 to 1939, then United States Attorney General from 1939 to 1940. Finally, in 1940, he was appointed by Roosevelt to the Supreme Court.

Murphy was known for being an early supporter of civil rights. As a trial judge, he presided over the trial of Ossian Sweet, a black doctor who had shot and killed one of a group of white men threatening his home. Murphy's dissenting argument in *Korematsu v. United States* reflects his view that the United States has a duty to treat all its citizens fairly.

Dissenting Opinion in the Case of *Korematsu v. United States*

Mr. Justice Murphy, dissenting.

This exclusion of 'all persons of Japanese ancestry, both **alien** and non-alien,' from the Pacific Coast area on a plea of military necessity in the absence of **martial law** ought not to be approved. Such exclusion goes over 'the very brink of constitutional power' and falls into the ugly **abyss** of racism.

In dealing with matters relating to the prosecution and progress of a war, we must **accord** great respect and consideration to the judgments of the military authorities who are on the scene and who have full knowledge of the military facts. The scope of their **discretion** must, as a matter of necessity and common sense, be wide. And their judgments ought not to be overruled lightly by those whose training and duties ill-equip them to deal intelligently with matters so **vital** to the physical security of the nation.

What is the rhetorical purpose of this paragraph?

At the same time, however, it is essential that there be definite limits to military discretion, especially where martial law has not been declared. Individuals must not be left impoverished of their constitutional rights on a plea of military necessity that has neither substance nor support. Thus, like other claims conflicting with the asserted constitutional rights of the individual, the military claim must subject itself to the judicial process of having its reasonableness determined and its conflicts with other interests reconciled. 'What are the allowable limits of military discretion, and whether or not they have been overstepped in a particular case, are **judicial** questions.'

This brief statement encapsulates Murphy's main point. Rephrase the statement in your own words.

The judicial test of whether the Government, on a plea of military necessity, can validly deprive an individual of any of his constitutional rights is whether the deprivation is reasonably related to a public danger that is so 'immediate, **imminent**, and **impending**' as not to admit of delay and not to permit the intervention of ordinary constitutional processes to alleviate the danger. Civilian Exclusion Order No. 34, banishing from a prescribed area of the Pacific Coast 'all persons of Japanese ancestry, both alien and non-alien,' clearly

How does Murphy develop his main point?

does not meet that test. Being an obvious racial discrimination, the order deprives all those within its scope of the equal protection of the laws as guaranteed by the Fifth Amendment. It further deprives these individuals of their constitutional rights to live and work where they will, to establish a home where they choose and to move about freely. In **excommunicating** them without benefit of hearings, this order also deprives them of all their constitutional rights to procedural due process. Yet no reasonable relation to an 'immediate, imminent, and impending' public danger is evident to support this racial restriction which is one of the most sweeping and complete deprivations of constitutional rights in the history of this nation in the absence of martial law.

It must be conceded that the military and naval situation in the spring of 1942 was such as to generate a very real fear of invasion of the Pacific Coast, accompanied by fears of sabotage and **espionage** in that area. The military command was therefore justified in adopting all reasonable means necessary to combat these dangers. In **adjudging** the military action taken in light of the then apparent dangers, we must not erect too high or too **meticulous** standards; it is necessary only that the action have some reasonable relation to the removal of the dangers of invasion, sabotage and espionage. But the exclusion, either temporarily or permanently, of all persons with Japanese blood in their veins has no such reasonable relation. And that relation is lacking because the exclusion order necessarily must rely for its reasonableness upon the assumption that all persons of Japanese ancestry may have a dangerous tendency to commit sabotage and espionage and to aid our Japanese enemy in other ways. It is difficult to believe that reason, logic or experience could be **marshaled** in support of such an assumption.

That this forced exclusion was the result in good measure of this **erroneous** assumption of racial guilt rather than **bona fide** military necessity is evidenced by the Commanding General's Final Report on the evacuation from the Pacific Coast area. In it he refers to all individuals of Japanese descent as '**subversive**,' as

Why does the exclusion order not have "reasonable relation" to the removal of danger?

belonging to 'an enemy race' whose 'racial strains are **undiluted**,' and as constituting 'over 112,000 potential enemies ... at large today' along the Pacific Coast. In support of this blanket condemnation of all persons of Japanese descent, however, no reliable evidence is cited to show that such individuals were generally disloyal, or had generally so conducted themselves in this area as to constitute a special menace to defense installations or war industries, or had otherwise by their behavior furnished reasonable ground for their exclusion as a group.

Justification for the exclusion is sought, instead, mainly upon questionable racial and sociological grounds not ordinarily within the realm of expert military judgment, supplemented by certain semi-military conclusions drawn from an unwarranted use of circumstantial evidence. Individuals of Japanese ancestry are condemned because they are said to be 'a large, **unassimilated**, tightly knit racial group, bound to an enemy nation by strong ties of race, culture, custom and religion.' They are claimed to be given to 'emperor worshipping ceremonies' and to 'dual citizenship.' Japanese language schools and allegedly pro-Japanese organizations are cited as evidence of possible group disloyalty, together with facts as to certain persons being educated and residing at length in Japan. It is intimated that many of these individuals deliberately resided '**adjacent** to strategic points,' thus enabling them 'to carry into execution a tremendous program of sabotage on a mass scale should any considerable number of them have been inclined to do so.' The need for protective custody is also asserted. The report refers without identity to 'numerous incidents of violence' as well as to other admittedly unverified or cumulative incidents. From this, plus certain other events not shown to have been connected with the Japanese Americans, it is concluded that the 'situation was fraught with danger to the Japanese population itself' and that the general public 'was ready to take matters into its own hands.' Finally, it is intimated, though not directly charged or proved, that persons of Japanese ancestry were responsible for three minor isolated shellings and bombings of the Pacific Coast area, as well as for unidentified radio transmissions and night signaling.

What evidence does Murphy provide? How does it support his main argument?

How do Murphy's language and use of specific quotes contribute to his main point?

The main reasons relied upon by those responsible for the forced evacuation; therefore, do not prove a reasonable relation between the group characteristics of Japanese Americans and the dangers of invasion, sabotage and espionage. The reasons appear, instead, to be largely an accumulation of much of the misinformation, half-truths and insinuations that for years have been directed against Japanese Americans by people with racial and economic prejudices—the same people who have been among the foremost advocates of the evacuation. A military judgment based upon such racial and sociological considerations is not entitled to the great weight ordinarily given the judgments based upon strictly military considerations. Especially is this so when every charge relative to race, religion, culture, geographical location, and legal and economic status has been substantially discredited by independent studies made by experts in these matters.

According to Murphy, the evacuation order is based on a logical error. Describe the error in your own words.

The military necessity which is essential to the validity of the evacuation order thus resolves itself into a few intimations that certain individuals actively aided the enemy, from which it is inferred that the entire group of Japanese Americans could not be trusted to be or remain loyal to the United States. No one denies, of course, that there were some disloyal persons of Japanese descent on the Pacific Coast who did all in their power to aid their ancestral land. Similar disloyal activities have been engaged in by many persons of German, Italian and even more pioneer stock in our country. But to infer that examples of individual disloyalty prove group disloyalty and justify discriminatory action against the entire group is to deny that under our system of law individual guilt is the sole basis for **deprivation** of rights. Moreover, this inference, which is at the very heart of the evacuation orders, has been used in support of the **abhorrent** and despicable treatment of minority groups by the dictatorial tyrannies which this nation is now pledged to destroy. To give constitutional sanction to that inference in this case, however well—intentioned may have been the military command on the Pacific Coast, is to adopt one of the cruelest of the rationales used by our enemies to destroy the dignity of the individual and to encourage and open the door to discriminatory actions against other minority groups in the passions of tomorrow. No adequate reason is given for the failure to treat these Japanese Americans on an individual basis by holding investigations and hearings to separate the loyal from the disloyal, as was done in the case of persons of German and Italian ancestry. It is asserted merely that the loyalties of this group 'were unknown and time was of the essence.' Yet nearly four months elapsed after Pearl Harbor before the first exclusion order was issued; nearly eight months went by until the last order was issued; and the last of these 'subversive' persons was not actually removed until almost eleven months had elapsed. Leisure and deliberation seem to have been more of the essence than speed. And the fact that conditions were not such as to warrant a declaration of martial law adds strength to the belief that the factors of time and military necessity were not as urgent as they have been represented to be.

Moreover, there was no adequate proof that the Federal Bureau of Investigation and the military and naval intelligence services did not have the espionage and sabotage situation well in hand during this long period. Nor is there any denial of the fact that not one person of Japanese ancestry was accused or convicted of espionage or sabotage after Pearl Harbor while they were still free, a fact which is some evidence of the loyalty of the vast majority of these individuals and of the effectiveness of the established methods of combatting these evils. It seems incredible that under these circumstances it would have been impossible to hold loyalty hearings for the mere 112,000 persons involved—or at least for the 70,000 American citizens-especially when a large part of this number represented children and elderly men and women. Any inconvenience that may have accompanied an attempt to conform to procedural due process cannot be said to justify violations of constitutional rights of individuals.

I dissent, therefore, from this legalization of racism. Racial discrimination in any form and in any degree has no justifiable part whatever in our democratic way of life.

◀ What, according to Murphy, is the inevitable outcome of the exclusion order's logic?

◀ How does Murphy frame this as a moral issue?

It is unattractive in any setting but it is utterly revolting among a free people who have embraced the principles set forth in the Constitution of the United States. All residents of this nation are **kin** in some way by blood or culture to a foreign land. Yet they are primarily and necessarily a part of the new and distinct civilization of the United States. They must accordingly be treated at all times as the heirs of the American experiment and as entitled to all the rights and freedoms guaranteed by the Constitution.

VOCABULARY

Note: All definitions are based on the context in which the term is used in this reading selection.

abhorrent: inspiring disgust or loathing

abyss: a deep and seemingly bottomless hole

accord: to grant or give as due

adjacent: next to or close to something else

adjudging: determining to be true through judicial power

alien: a person of foreign descent

bona fide: genuine or real

deprivation: the act of being deprived; being without something considered to be a necessity

discretion: freedom of choice

erroneous: wrong or incorrect

espionage: the act of spying to obtain information, usually from governmental operations

excommunicating: depriving the right of membership or inclusion

imminent: likely to occur in the near future

impending: threatening to happen or occur soon

judicial: related to the proper courts of law

kin: related by blood

marshaled: gathered; assembled

martial law: military governance over a civilian population during a time of unrest

meticulous: showing great attention to detail; precise

subversive: liable to undermine or overthrow a government; treasonous

unassimilated: not integrated or absorbed into a society

undiluted: free from extraneous elements; unmixed

vital: very important; pertinent

EXERCISES

Answer each of the following questions in a few sentences, based on the text you have just read. Briefly explain each of your answers.

1. How, according to Murphy, does the battle between military and judicial authority play out in the exclusion order?

2. Explain Murphy's reasoning regarding individuals vs. groups. Cite specific passages that back up this argument.

3. Explain how the seventh paragraph refines the idea of the plea of military necessity without support introduced in the third paragraph.

4. White farmers in California saw Japanese farmers as a danger to their business interests; they lobbied for restrictions on immigration. There is some evidence that these farmers were at least partly behind the effort to remove Japanese people from the area. How does Murphy suggest and support the idea that the motivation for the exclusion order was not really military, but political and economic?

5. How does Murphy frame racism, and, by extension, the exclusion order, as a moral issue for the United States?

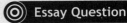 **Essay Question**

Compare the language of Justice Murphy's argument to that of "The Death of Captain Waskow." How is each typical of its respective genre? Cite specific details in your answer.